T0193684

A
Caregiver's
Heart,
Hands,
and
Health

DOROTHY J. MCDANIEL

WESTBOW
PRESS®
A DIVISION OF THOMAS NELSON
& ZONDERVAN

WestBow Press books may be ordered through booksellers or by contacting:

WestBow Press
A Division of Thomas Nelson & Zondervan
1663 Liberty Drive
Bloomington, IN 47403
www.westbowpress.com
1 (866) 928-1240

Scripture quotations KJV taken from the King James Version of the Bible.

ISBN: 978-1-9736-6670-7 (sc)
ISBN: 978-1-9736-6696-7 (hc)
ISBN: 978-1-9736-6671-4 (e)

Library of Congress Control Number: 2019908334

Print information available on the last page.

WestBow Press rev. date: 6/28/2019

To my late parents, James Edward Jr. and Victoria Phillip Whittaker, who taught me moral values and to love God and my siblings.

To my late husband, William Earl McDaniel Sr., who is greatly missed. He was my greatest supporter and cheerleader. His love continues to inspire me to reach higher heights and deeper depths in the Word of God.

To my siblings: my brother and his wife, Elders Irvin and Minnie Whittaker; and my sisters, Shirley, Evelyn, Lucinda, and Stella. To all my children, grands, and great-grands, thank you all for your prayers and support to the ministry. I love you all.

To all the Intercessor Prayer Warriors, who participate and uphold me in prayer, God bless you all. To all the facilitators who minister the Word on the prayer line, I thank the Lord for each of you. I want to thank Minister Sharon Davis for assistance in the initial phase of this publication. A very special thanks to Elder Janice King, who is a personal asset to the ministry and was instrumental in the implementation of the Miracles of Faith Prayer Line.

To caregivers all over the world. I pray that they be strengthened with all might as they minister to others.

Finally, but most importantly, to our Lord and Savior Jesus Christ, who inspires me and made this venture possible. To God be all the glory, honor, dominion, and power, forever and ever. Amen.

CONTENTS

ACKNOWLEDGMENTS

I wish to thank our children: Edward Earl, Annette, Judy, William Earl Jr., Linda, Joy, Regina, Dion, and Robin, for their devotion and support to the ministry. To my many surrogate sons and daughters I am grateful for you as well.

I'm thankful to God for Mrs. Geneva Berry, my former nurse manager, Elder Lula Newkirk, my Assistant Director of nursing services at Medical Park Nursing Center, and many others; of whom I've had the pleasure of working and interacting with.

INTRODUCTION

I am a retired registered nurse who was afforded the opportunity to be a professional caregiver for fifty years. I became the personal caregiver to my mother, Victoria Whittaker, and to my late husband, William Earl McDaniel, for ten years.

I have opted to become the voice and spokesperson for many other caregivers all over the world, due to my personal experiences and insight in rendering care to others. My goal for writing this book is to address the important roles of caregivers;

to make others aware of the pros and cons that could impact their heart, hands, and their health; and to encourage all caregivers, whether their service is provided in homes or institutions. Regardless of the venue, the roles they provide as caregivers are vitally important to the maintenance and well-being of others. The issues addressed in this book are not all inclusive of the plights of all caregivers, nor of their personal experiences, but serve as a basic overview of what caregivers encounter and experience.

CHAPTER 1

Ministry of Caregivers

Caregiving is a ministry ordained by God that requires hands on the recipient. While rendering care to others, many caregivers experience physical strains and emotional stresses that affect their lives.

Caregivers are unsung heroes who often put their dreams, goals, and attention to themselves on hold while devoting their lives to care for others. The following scriptures serve to encourage all caregivers.

"For God is not unrighteous to forget your labor of Love, which you have shown toward

His Name, in that you have ministered to the saints, and do minister" (Hebrews 6:10).

> "Then shall the righteous answer Him, Lord, when saw we Thee an hungered, and fed Thee? Or thirsty and gave Thee drink when saw we Thee a stranger, and took Thee in? or naked and clothed Thee? Or when saw we sick or in prison and came unto Thee? And the King shall answer and say unto them, verily I say unto you, inasmuch as ye have done it unto one of the least of these My

brethren, you have done it unto Me". (Matthew 25:37–40)

We All Have Basic Needs

According to Maslow's Hierarchy of needs, we all have the inherent need for love, a feeling of belonging, safety, and socialization. We knowingly and unknowingly seek to have these needs met on a daily basis.

Caregivers Serve as Role Models

Caregivers serve as role models to others in families, churches, and communities as they demonstrate, through their actions, that it is more blessed to give than to receive. Case in point upon my completing nursing school many others were inspired to become caregivers.

The Word of God says,

> "I have shown you all things, how that so laboring ye sought to support the weak, and to remember the words of The Lord Jesus, how He said, 'It is more blessed to give than to receive'" (Acts 20:35).

CHAPTER 2

Caregivers Categorized

As a caregiver in the home and a registered nurse in several facilities, I have observed three basic types of caregivers.

1. **Model** caregivers are patient, ***compassionate, kindhearted***, and ***empathetic***, and ***show unconditional love*** to all recipients, regardless of race, creed, or nationality. This category reflects the Word of God, which says,

"And as you would that men should do to you, do ye also to them likewise" (Luke 6:31).

2. **In-home** caregivers have the *heart of the model caregiver*, but *health issues* prevent them from providing optimum physical care to others. This situation causes stress and anxiety for both parties involved. Although there are resources in the community to assist, there may be a lengthy process for the recipient to receive benefits.

3. **Careless hearts** have *good health and available hands*, but *do not have the heart, the patience, or the mind-set* to

render care in the home or an institution. In my opinion, the people in this group could be opportunistic, insubordinate, and hateful. These individuals could also exhibit abusive, neglectful behavior toward recipients. Some of the caregivers in this category could very well be family members who have not had the education or training on how to properly care for the elderly or sick. Regardless of the reason, this type of behavior is unacceptable.

CHAPTER 3

In-Home Care versus Institutional Care

S ome caregivers opt to care for people in the home who have various chronic debilitating diseases and conditions because they feel an obligation to the individual or they don't trust others to give adequate care. Some may need the income from the recipient to assist in maintaining the household, which can be very costly. Elderly caregivers are reluctant to place the chronically ill person in an institution due to not having transportation or the ability to visit their loved one as often as they would desire.

Therefore, they keep him or her at home as long as they can, with the assumption that no one else will treat the recipient like they will.

Be mindful that there is a distinct difference between caregiving in the home and in an institution. Institutional care is managed and supervised, with duties being assigned by management. In the home, some caregivers have the sole responsibility to care for others, even as their own health is often compromised, which definitely affects their heart and hands.

Institutional care provides professional overall care around the clock and provides adequate nutrition, medication, and an obligation to meet the patient's overall health needs. Institutional care is beneficial but lacks one-on-one attention due to large caseloads.

Stressed While Giving Care

Stress is a major factor in a caregiver's life. Many caregivers are plagued with illnesses related to stress, which in turn affects every organ in their bodies, making them vulnerable to heart problems, cancer, diabetes, and other physical, emotional, and mental disorders. Many caregivers' immune systems are compromised from lack of sufficient rest, poor eating habits, and lack of medical interventions.

CHAPTER 4

A Caregiver's Personal Testimony

As a child reared in the rural area of Carroll County, Mississippi, I dreamed of becoming a nurse when I grew up. The longing in my heart did not come from mentoring or from knowing a real nurse; the seed was planted by my father's vision for my life.

He would often say to my mother in my presence, "Dorothy is going to be a registered nurse, and she will take care of us in our old age." Little did I know that his prophecy would become a beautiful reality. The word of God says,

For verily I say unto you, That whosoever shall say unto this mountain, Be thou removed and be thou cast into the sea; and shall not doubt in his heart, but shall believe that those things which he saith shall come to pass; he shall have whatsoever he saith. (Mark 11:23)

My dad encouraged all of his children to strive for excellence in education. As a result, I became an avid reader, who sought to learn all I could about the medical profession. Although my access to reading material was limited, especially regarding nursing, I read anything that pertained to the medical field.

I was naive back then about the nursing profession. I thought each nurse had to work around the clock. I would say to myself, "I don't know how I can work both day and night, but if anyone else can do it, I can do it too. The Lord will give me strength to do it!" I believe God smiled and winked at my naivete. He saw the sincerity of my heart, and provided a way for me to fulfill his purpose and granted me the desire of my heart.

After I completed high school, my dad took me to take an aptitude test for entrance in the Practical nurse program at Mississippi Vocational College. I could hardly sleep that night. I was filled with a mixture of emotions, including excitement, anticipation, and nervousness. I was nervous because I had no idea what an aptitude test was or what it consisted of. In spite of my emotions, I was glad to have the opportunity to fulfill my lifelong dream to become a nurse.

I got up early that morning to go take the test, which was given at the employment office in the town of Greenwood, Mississippi, a few miles from Teoc. I was a bit apprehensive, not knowing what to expect, and my apprehension intensified when I realized I was the only young (17 years old) female, who was in a room with two other white men. I was approached by the white, male tester, who appeared to be about six feet tall, over two hundred pounds, and very hostile. As he instructed me about the test, in a very hateful condescending tone, his chin shook like a big bowl of jello. He did not greet me but handed me the testing materials. In a very deep gruff voice he told me to fill out the papers and that the test would be timed. It seemed to me he didn't believe I would be able to complete the test in time.

I did as I was told, no questions asked, and met the required time frame. After completing the test, I felt pretty sure I had passed the written portion. But then the same gruffed-voice man came back with a board and some pegs to check my dexterity.

He directed me to place the pegs in the slots on the board as fast as I could, because this test was timed as well.

Now I was really nervous, as I thought that I might not pass this portion of the test. The thought of disappointing my dad and missing out on getting into the nursing program at Mississippi Vocational College was too much to bear. With all these thoughts going through my mind, I stumbled placing the pegs on the board. The mean old tester showed no emotion or any kindness. In truth, he got angry and seemed frustrated with me when I fumbled. He seemed to think that I was an inanimate object that he had to painstakingly deal with during his daily routine. He showed no compassion or human emotion toward me.

Finally, he turned and said to a man nearby, "They are getting worse and worse. This one will never make it."

The other man asked, "What does she want to do?"

The first man answered in a disgusting undertone, as if I were nowhere in the room, "She wants to be a nurse." I was silent but internalized what was being said.

When I completed the tests, the tester never said a word to me. He told my dad, "She barely made it."

My dad answered, "As long as she passed, that's good enough for me!"

I was so glad that I had not disappointed my dad and that I would be enrolled in the nursing program. But the negative words of the tester continued to replay in my mind. "She will never make it!" That negative phrase lit a fire in my spirit; I was determined to make him a liar.

Upon entering the preclinical nursing program, I excelled and made straight A's!

My classmates nicknamed me "The Brain." They sneered and poked fun at the fact that I was determined to excel and didn't take part in their slothful ways. Their remarks did not interrupt my determination to succeed.

Upon finishing preclinical rotation, I went to Vicksburg, Mississippi, for my clinical training at Kuhn Memorial Hospital. I graduated in 1959, passing the state boards the first time, and became a licensed practical nurse. I was the only one in my class of ten who passed. I felt badly for them, but I praised the Lord that I had passed.

I worked eighteen years as an LPN (licensed practical nurse). I then went back to nursing school in 1976, at James Sprunt Community College, and became a licensed registered nurse in 1978—a lifelong dream for me and my family. My dad said, "This is the highlight of my life." I became the first black director of nursing services in a long-term care facility in the eastern North Carolina area. All praises belong to God!

In 1984, I was promoted to director of nursing services at Medical Park Nursing Center in Mount Olive, North Carolina. I always had a passion for helping hurting people. Perhaps I became more emphatic about my career, as I witnessed my grandfather die from complications of diabetes. It strengthened my resolve to alleviate suffering for people within the scope of my nursing practice.

CHAPTER 5

The Caregiver's Heart

There are caregivers who encounter many dilemmas that not only affect their heart but their health. There are situations and circumstances whereby the caregiver's positive plan can end in disastrous results. This is a true story that I encountered while caring for my husband and my mother.

I was the express caregiver for my aged mother and my invalid husband. I had been encouraging my husband to go to church with me and my mother, even though both had just had major operations. Earl, my husband, had just had an above-the-knee amputation, and my mother had a knee replacement. I felt it would be good for them to get out of the house. After much convincing, they consented. So I got them dressed to go to church.

I approached the church and saw all the cars that I realized that today was not an ordinary service but a Union service, where many churches in a district come together to worship at one church on fifth Sunday. I didn't want to go back home after all the trouble I had gone through to get them ready, so I parked the car and assisted both of them from the car into their wheelchairs. The church was filled to capacity. The ushers and I had to take them all the way to the front of the church. My mother was seated up front with the mothers of the church, and my husband was seated up front with the deacons. With his recent amputation, Earl didn't like the idea of being in front.

The service was in full bloom when I saw my husband, Earl, frowning and almost at the point of tears. I motioned from across the room and mouthed, "What's wrong?"

He whispered, "I'm about to freeze. I'm sitting over the air-conditioner vent." His physician had prescribed blood-thinning medication, so I began to panic, trying to figure out how I was going to help him because the area where he was sitting was so congested. Furthermore, it was hot in the church, so I didn't want to ask the usher to turn off the air-conditioner. I had to do something fast to help him without interrupting the preacher's sermon. I prayed because I didn't know anything else to do.

I looked at Earl; he was shivering, and his teeth were chattering. I said, "Oh, Lord, you got to help him with this one!" My mind was spinning. Then I saw an usher. I called him over and told him to go shut off the vent underneath my husband's wheelchair.

He did so, but Earl whispered, "It's still coming through!" I called the usher again and told him to find some books to place over the vent under Earl's wheelchair. He did as I asked, which made Earl comfortable enough to remain for the duration of the service. Needless to say, I could not concentrate on the message that was preached because I was so absorbed in watching my husband and mother during the service. Both she and my husband were depending upon me for their total care. I was so absorbed by and attuned to my husband's discomfort. It was as if I could feel the bone-chilling cold that he was experiencing, and my chief aim was to promote comfort and restore a feeling of well-being in both their lives. I was relieved when service dismissed that Sunday, to say the least.

A true caregiver's heart is receptive to the feelings of the client and responds respectively. It is important to triage the need of each one and render care according to the priority of needs. This often causes the caregiver to neglect or delay attending to their own personal needs. Therefore, many health issues are often ignored until they become grave in nature.

CHAPTER 6

The Caregiver's Hands

Being a caregiver to someone in the home is much more intense than rendering care on a professional level in an institution. This is especially so if the receiver of the care is a family member. The caregiver takes on the receiver's persona and becomes the eyes, ears, and spokesperson for that individual. The caregiver anticipates, plans for, and meets the needs of the individual based on their mental and physical conditions. In other words, caregivers provide for the recipient as though they were the recipient of the care themselves.

Many caregivers function in multiple roles, which can sometimes be overwhelming. Some caregivers manage a household and work a full-time job in order to make ends meet. The caregiver has the responsibility of assuring balance in the life of the recipient, which includes providing optimum nutritional status for the individual. This might include spoon-feeding, adequate hydration, regular bowel and bladder eliminations, good skin care to prevent breakdown of skin tissue, frequent position changes, a safe environment to prevent falls, giving medication on time, ensuring that the medications are swallowed (since some might hide or throw the medications away), making appointments and assuring appointments are followed up with, providing assistance with mobility, and assuming total personal care as needed. Many caregivers' personal ideals and goals are placed on the back burner in order to fulfill their obligations as the primary care provider

It's almost impossible to separate the heart, hands, and health of caregivers, because all components are used in the process of caring for others.

The physical safety aspect of turning, lifting, transferring, and transporting those with mobility issues is of utmost importance and challenging for both. Many have sustained long-term, chronic damage to their backs and limbs by using improper techniques while transferring and caring for others. Aged clients are subject to frequent falls, and caregivers should know their own physical limitations and seek help for themselves as needed. This ensures their own safety and that of the recipient as well.

CHAPTER 7

The Caregiver's Health

Caregivers' health issues are often ignored. While I was caring for my aged mother and my husband, Earl, who was a double amputee with multiple health issues, I was diagnosed with Fuchs' corneal dystrophy, a condition of my left eye that caused my vision to become impaired. It grew progressively worse over time. I didn't tell my husband or my mother how serious my vision problem had become because they had enough problems of their own. I suffered in silence as I went about making their lives as normal and as comfortable as possible. I also worked a job part-time early on, which is what a lot of other caregivers do.

My husband had kidney failure and had to be taken to dialysis twice weekly. Some days, my sight was so impaired I couldn't tell the color of the signal light until I got right up to it. I would often ask my son the color of the light as I approached it. I was the only driver in the house, and I suffered from poor vision for years. It was only after my mother expired in 2009 and my husband expired in 2010 that I was able to have my vision restored with a corneal transplant in 2011.

The other health dilemma I faced had to deal with secondhand smoke. My husband was a chain-smoker; he had smoked cigarettes since his youth. His smoking had grossly compromised his circulatory system and his diabetic condition, which resulted in the double amputation of his legs. After ingesting his smoke for many years, it began to take its toll on my health. I began to have respiratory problems, congestion, and asthma-like symptoms, which required multiple medical interventions. The doctor told me my problem was the result of secondhand smoke, that I had to rid myself of it in order to remain healthy.

I tried to impress upon my husband that I could no longer be subjected to his smoking. He would try to comply by not smoking in my presence, but because of his addiction, it was hard for him to refrain from smoking altogether, and the whole house reeked of smoke. He smoked in the bed at night, until one night he set the bed and carpet on fire; that ended his smoking in bed. He then tried to be sensitive about his smoking habit, but smoke itself has no sensitivity to any particular person, so again I suffered through it all.

His lungs were so diseased that his doctor wanted him to have oxygen in the house to use at intervals, but he refused because he knew that he could not smoke while using oxygen. So we established separate sleeping quarters. This helped somewhat but didn't completely alleviate the problem. I could smell the smoke anytime he would light a cigarette. Even the walls in our home had a yellowish tint due to the smoke.

A friend's dad had been a chain-smoker, and his dog was his constant companion; his dog sat near him as he smoked. The dog finally died of lung cancer, and so did her dad shortly thereafter.

Many caregivers experience similar conditions and are neglectful of their own health in order to care for and serve others.

CHAPTER 8

The Caregiver's Stressors/Woes

S tress can be defined as strain or pressure on a person, physically or mentally. Caregivers often experience stress on a regular basis in dealing with others.

Stress is somewhat like a fire. When it is contained and controlled, it is beneficial. Only when the fire is not contained or controlled can it cause major destruction, so it is with stress. In small amounts, it is healthy and beneficial to an individual, but stress in abundance can cause multiple major mental and physical health issues.

Some stressors are caused by the caregiver experiencing the role reversal of caring for parents or a loved one. The individual who's normal role is caregiver becomes the one who now has to receive care. My mother called me mama in her latter years, and at times, my husband reverted to being a child. In addition some caregivers have the responsibility of caring for people with severe dementia or Alzheimer's which may include decline of memory, personality, and the ability to feed themselves and take care of their personal needs. These conditions could continue for years. Due to these factors the caregiver may experience a higher level of emotional stress. Which imposes a major burden on the caregiver and can affect every organ in their body.

One other stressor that the caregiver experiences is that of isolation. Many caregivers in the home feel a sense of abandonment. They don't have the support that is needed to give sufficient care. Many have been thrust into a caregiving role, and they receive little or no training for the care they are required to give. This places a great burden upon them physically, mentally, and spiritually.

Some caregivers have the benefit of long-distance supporters consisting of family and friends. These individuals sense the tremendous strain on the caregiver, and although they may not be able to visit as often as desired, their frequent calls, prayers, and financial assistance are great ways to share the burden and support the caregiver.

As I cared for our mother for nine years, my siblings and other relatives were far away and were as supportive as they could be from a distance. The frequent calls, prayers, and financial support were a great blessing. My brother, Irvin, sent a check each month for me to have a *me* day. That was a special blessing that I took full advantage of. My siblings realized that I had to have my needs met in order to function at my highest level and give our mother the best possible care.

Caregivers should take advantage of the support that is offered by family, friends, community resources, government agencies, and local churches. All of the above should be aware of the great work that is being done and the assistance being provided. Caregivers have been divinely commissioned to serve others in order to be successful in our mission. We must take good care of our bodies, guard our hearts, and exhibit much patience in order to render optimum care (service) to others as unto the Lord.

On one occasion, while managing a long-term nursing center, I was summoned to be at the bedside of a lady who was 103 years old. I recognized that she was expiring, so

I called her family to her bedside. I was led to read to her from the Holy Bible. I read slowly and consistently as her family quietly sat back and witnessed her transition, which was very peaceful and serene. As I gently led her into the arms of Jesus, I said, "Jesus's arms are open to receive you right now."

She made a deep sigh and went to sleep. Her family commented, "I have never seen anything like that before!" They were in awe of how peacefully she slipped away.

CHAPTER 9

The Caregiver's Reward

Caregivers are blessed to perform a role that's sanctioned by the Word of God:

> "I have shown you all things, how that so laboring ye ought to support the weak, and to remember the words of The Lord Jesus, how He said, 'It is more blessed to give than to receive'" (Acts 20:35).

Cheerfully, caregivers can be assured their roles are highly esteemed of God.

"For God Loveth a cheerful giver. And God is able to make all grace abound toward you, that ye, always having all sufficiency in all things may abound to every good work" (2 Corinthians 9:7–8).

What you make happen for others, God will richly reward you accordingly, as it is stated in the Word:

"For with the same measure that you meet withal it shall be measured to you again" (Luke 6:38b) and "And let's not be weary in well doing: for in due season we shall reap; if we faint not" (Galatians 6:9).

CHAPTER 10

The Caregiver's Final Reward

So, personal caregivers all over the world, know that the God of the universe will richly reward you for all your labors of love, as written in his Word:

> And before Him shall He gather all nations: and He shall separate them one from another, as a Shepherd divide His sheep from the goats and He shall set the sheep on His right Hand, but the goads on the left. Then shall The King say unto them

on the right Hand, come ye blessed of My Father, enter the Kingdom prepared for you from the foundation of the world: for I was hungry and you gave Me meat, I was thirsty and you gave Me drink, I was a stranger, and you took Me in, naked and you clothed Me, I was sick and ye visited Me, I was in prison and you came unto Me. Then shall the righteous say unto Him, saying, Lord when did I see You hungry and fed You? Or thirsty and gave You drink? When saw we Thee a stranger and took

You in? or naked and clothed You? When did we see You sick or in prison and came unto You? And The King shall answer and say unto them, Verily I say unto you, inasmuch as you have done it unto one of the least of these My brother, you have done it unto Me. (Matthew 25:37–40)

CHAPTER 11

Intercessory Prayer
for Caregivers

Father God, in Jesus's name, I come boldly to the throne of grace on behalf of caregivers all over the world. I ask that you impart a special blessing to each and every one of them. I pray that they love you with all of their heart first and then love others as you have loved us. Father, help them to be sensitive to the needs of those they encounter.

Father, strengthen their hands with all might to be able to carry out their God-given assignments. I pray that you bless the work of their hands. I pray, Father, that their hands will support the weak and minister to others, because it is written it is more blessed to give than to receive. I pray that everything their hands touch will prosper.

Father, create in each caregiver a clean heart and renew the right spirit within them. I pray you will open the eyes of their heart so they can be sensitive to meet the needs of others spiritually, mentally, and physically. Father God, give them the willingness to serve others as unto you. I pray you keep their hearts and minds through Jesus Christ our Lord, that they continue to do your will with all their heart.

Father, I pray that they be in good health and prosper even as their souls prosper. I pray no disease will come near their dwelling, that you give your angels charge over them in all their ways. In the name of Jesus, I bind the spirit of infirmity and disease that renders them powerless to carry out their assigned duties. I decree and declare no weapon formed against them shall be able to prosper. Help them to be sensitive to the prompting of your Holy Spirit, that their health spring forth speedily.

Father, I pray that you bless them in every area of their lives, that they will seek your face on a daily basis, to seek you first for divine guidance and direction for their lives and for the lives of others. I pray that they will cast all of their woes and cares on you because you are our burden bearer and heavy-load carrier.

Father, I pray that each and every one of these caregivers be saved and have a personal relationship with you, that they be filled with the Holy Spirit and allow your love, joy, and peace to lead and guide them forever. I pray you will give them a praying spirit. As it is written 2 Chronicles 7:14, "If my people which are called by name shall humble themselves, and pray, and seek my face, and turn from their wicked ways; then will I hear from heaven will forgive their sins and will heal their land."

Father, I pray the spirit of the Lord will give them wisdom and revelation knowledge to heighten their discernment. Help them to be quick to hear, slow to speak, and slow to anger. Let them be merciful, tenderhearted, and patient while giving grace to others and loving unconditionally as you have loved us. I pray that the blood of Jesus saturate them from the crown of their head to the soles of their feet. I pray that they will be lenders and not borrowers, to be the head and not the tail.

We ask all of these blessings in the majestic name of Jesus the Christ. Amen!

ABOUT THE AUTHOR

Dorothy Jean Whittaker McDaniel was born November 2, 1939, in Carroll County, Mississippi. She is the daughter of the late James Edward Jr. and the late Victoria P. Whittaker, and is the fifth of nine children.

She was married to the late William Earl McDaniel Sr. She is a mother, grandmother, and a great-grandmother. She resides in Mt. Olive, North Carolina, and is a retired registered nurse after working for fifty years in the nursing service in various capacities.

Mrs. McDaniel, "Ms. Mc" as she is so lovingly called, was the first black director of nursing services in a long-term nursing facility in the eastern area of North Carolina.

She is an Evangelist who was called by God to minister the Word in 1986. She is an associate elder at Gospel Light United Holy Church of America in Mt. Olive, North Carolina, where the presiding pastor is Dr. Dwight Morrissey Sr.

Evangelist McDaniel is the founder of Miracles of Faith Ministry, Incorporated (M.O.F.) of Mt. Olive, North Carolina. Miracles of Faith Ministry, Inc. encompasses a twenty-four-hour intercessory prayer wheel with a conference prayer line. It operates

Monday through Friday from 6:00 a.m. to 7:00 a.m., Monday evenings from 6:00 p.m. to 7:00 p.m., and Thursdays at noon. The prayer line is open each Sunday morning from 8:30 a.m. to 8:45 a.m. as she ministers on the local radio station WDJS 1430 AM while simultaneously being on the prayer line. To access the prayer line, call (213) 936-8596, enter access code 680933, and press #.

Miracles of Faith Ministry, Inc. has hosted three eight-hour prayer vigils / shut-ins from 10:00 p.m. to 6:00 a.m. in December 2016, 2017, and hosted a Holy Spirit Power-Filled Prayer Conference on December 1, 2018.

The Miracles of Faith Ministry, Inc. (MOF) has an actual prayer house where Elder McDaniel ministers, Monday evenings and on Thursdays at noon, located at 709 South Chestnut Street, Mt. Olive, North Carolina.

The MOF ministry serves Meals-on-Wheels to the elderly, sick, and shut-in every third Saturday of the month. The meals are prepared by evangelist McDaniel and are transported into the local community with assistance from her family and other volunteers.

Evangelist McDaniel does a visiting ministry to the sick in the community and in institutions as well. She has published two books, *Supernatural Encounters*, published in 2006, and *Wake Up the Sleeping Giants*, published in 2014. This publication is the third book, and the fourth book is coming!

She attended William Carter Christian College and the United Christian College, in Goldsboro, North Carolina. She continues to study to show herself approved unto the Lord.

Her nursing education took place at Mississippi Vocational College in Ittabena, Mississippi; James Sprunt Community College in Kenansville, North Carolina; and East Carolina University in Greenville, North Carolina.

She enjoys traveling, reading, writing, cooking, watching *Jeopardy* and basketball games.

Her godly wisdom, counsel, and nursing expertise have made her a valuable asset to her family, church, and community.

Printed in the United States
By Bookmasters